Odyssey in the Making

Jen Selinsky

Kindle Direct Publishing

ISBN 9798652771553

*Not every poem included in this book is dated in chronological order. This is not an oversight on my part. Rather, I have made changes and substitutions over the years.

-J.L.S.

You are driving me to the brink
Of insanity, anticipating what
Should be a victory.
All in a moment's hesitation,
My breath quickens, and my heart
Seems to stop.
I can't take much more, as
Endorphins rush out all over
My body, and my vital signs
Of life turn to rage.
Defenseless in this situation;
I hate not being able to
Control my fate!

12/20/04

In the Wake of the Storm

Best stay away, lest I use
My forces against you—turn
Your insides out right
Before your eyes!
Oh, beware my power as
You take heed.
Beware! This night and
For the rest of your life,
When you can see the
Hurricane in my eyes, which
Means I am about to descend
On those who antagonize me.

12/20/04

Blood running down the walls
At such a costly demise.
I can no longer see a compromise
Because their fate is sealed—
Designed to make a mockery
Of what I stand for, what
I have loved as my own brethren.
Now, I am forced to take a
Defeatist attitude and
Resign to remain locked
In my room, where I can do no harm.
Heart pumping mad,
Veins tensing, but I do
Not care!
Let me at whatever angers
Me so they know to
No longer push me over the
Edge at such a cruel
Defeat that I felt it deep in my heart.
A piece of my life was cut off
And tossed into the bonfire—ridiculed by the
Worst and, now, I can feel

The beast awakening inside—
So prominent that I am
Beginning to scare even myself.
Bah! So why should I care
What the world thinks
Now that they have
Seen my exterior shine.
Under so many different lights?
I have done no better—no worse
To surpass the laughter echoing
Inside my head.
Loving me, yet teasing me
At the same time.
My dear, now truly you can see
The inside of my head—
Streams of ember spewing
Out of my mouth, so much
That even immortal creatures become afraid.
Bitter heart refuses to let go of this fantasy,
But I derive so much pleasure from
Forming words out of anger, words that
Define my very character.

Oh, back to the crushing blow,
As someone mentions it again;
It stirs the blood back up
And causes me to lose what
Little control that I had to begin with.
Oh, why does this hurt so much;
Why do these scathing remarks taunt me,
As I feel like breaking the silence
With a pained yell, a cry of rage,
If you will.
The tips of my fingers becoming very hot,
As they make their impressions on the page,
Ready to burn a hole right through
At any instant!
To make use of the fire to go outside
And melt all the ice—a blazing inferno,
As I walk up and down the familiar streets,
With such a vengeance that would
Make Lamia seem like nothing.
Tears welling up inside, the other part of me
Wants to cry—weakness causing me
To sink to my knees as my bloodied fists

Pound the cold pavement.
To naught (fear not)
Like the poor, innocent nut
Being crushed with the
Pressure of my fist,
Looming because my rage is something
That I cannot resist.
This has driven me to the point
That I want to fight the tranquility
That's trying to set in—fight like my brethren
Against someone who should not be such
The cause of my distress, but, o', those
Damned voices won't let it quit, as I can
Imagine what people may say, people who
Innocently tease and do not know
The full extent of my wrath.
It's an abomination, nonetheless!
So I sequester myself, as
Long as I can, to ensure
The safety of my fellow man.
How long this will take;
I do not know—enough time

To allow my cynicism to flow.

12/21/04

Almost

At a complete loss for words
And any other (thoughts)
Because nothing else matters
At this moment; nothing can
Break my concentration.
My cool-headed counterparts
Reside downstairs—all around
Me, to hose me down, when
My body temperature rises
To an alarming red.
I will let no one come
Near me now, when something
Is still severely wrong.

12/21/04

Damn all this,
Enough cause for anger
To turn me into
The most feared monster,
Who can overturn
Buildings with ease.

12/21/04

Now that time has allowed me
To be smooth, I can let myself out.
Let me to go see how I deal
With the world.
Depression still lodged in my heart,
Even though, I know, the wound
Is going to be healed, sooner or later.
But, let me hear no more of it,
Lest I get some of the anger back
A small beast still lies within me.

12/21/04

Western Sunset

How do the people out there feel
With the final sun shining down—
Golden orange with the slightly cool wind
Blowing against their backs?
(It's) as if the tranquil atmosphere
Just beckons them to sleep,
Slowly and ever so peacefully.
They can feel their limbs getting heavier,
As the beautiful colors fuse with
Their hair.

12/21/04

Constant state of circumstance
And the people who refuse to
Let me be myself;
I want to make sure
That their tyranny is put to an end!
Why fear?
I can't help it because it's part of
My nature.
All my life, I have had conflicts
Such as these.
When will they go away
(Actually, I pose thing question
As an "if.")
Yes, you are going, and
I am coming in
The other door while these spectators
Are chasing my illusion
Across the false yard.
All these frightening
Images threaten you
To cease to be—
Cease to reside in my head.

Ah yes, they shall disappear
Right before whatever happens
To be present, and those who have
Crossed the storm will greatly
Rue their decision.

12/22/04

I need no progeny,
Sprung from my lions,
As proof of my existence.
I need no daily struggle,
Nor regret.
All the necessary components
Reside inside my head.
Heart-to-brain-to-hand,
Pen to paper.
My legacy will not be
Restricted to family—
Words will flow in the blood of
Strangers of future generations,
And my name will last
With the dawn of each new day!

12/23/04

Unfamiliar Territory

Sometimes, I feel as though
I am on shaky ground, even though
I know I am in good company.
These people, how will they
Correspond to my needs & do
They know of the background
That has recently followed behind?
Here comes the claim to my nerves.

12/23/04

Now comes forth the beauty
That has shone in the
Prophetic skies.
Such a delight, so many
At a time witnessed.
You have seen devotion
Coming through on my part
All during the chosen times.
Here come the words to speak
In what I feel to be joy.

12/23/04

When once you took it upon yourself
To devote our love in something
That would make even the most
Immortal being green with envy;
We would roam the great woodlands—
The cushiony snow supporting our footsteps,
As we embark upon a short journey
To our secret retreat.
What happened to those days; were they
Really so long ago?
It seems that Time has
Forgotten our ways—
Forgotten the very grace which we
Presented to all those around.
Oh, Love! Can we
Not return to those days
That beckon our names all over
Inside my head?
Would you find no comfort in recapturing
A falling star?
Such is the very thing
That I would like

To do before the final iceberg falls from
Our haven (we) created.

12/23/04

Prayers
And thoughts
Illustrated in our heads
Fall into our stream
Of consciousness,
When we least expect
Their doings.
In a moment's hesitation,
I wake from a hopeful slumber
And discover that my spirit
Has connected with the physical
Component of my mind.
And who knows what sometimes
Triggers these thoughts, fragments
From yesterday's conversation?
The answer can only come to me in my sleep.

12/23/04

Such a majestic beauty on strings;
I wish that I could hear your words
Sung out loud and clear—
Sung out so that no man can
Any longer misunderstand.
I suppose that my wish cannot be granted
At this precise moment, but I can always
Imagine from what I have in my head.

12/23/04

Part of my mind
Cannot believe
That this splendid holiday
Will come to us soon—
Merely hours away.
When was the last time
I fully embraced the meaning,
At least part of what it's
Supposed to mean?
Oh, but I have had
Such an opportunity
To give, yes, let my gifts
Please those
Who've the fortune
Of receiving from what I was
Able to give.
Such an inner joy
From presenting outward
In such a fashion.
No matter! Let me
Not lose my heart.
Please have my life arranged

According to plan,

As long as benevolence

Still rests comfortably

In the generous space

Inside my heart.

12/23/04

“A penny for your thoughts,”
Someone might say, in case
You have not heard the
Phrase before.
They know, everyone has to
Know that something is on my mind—
Has been on my mind since the
Creation of my being.
Oh, when I cease to think
I shall no longer be!
Such a life would not exist
Because this organ must make
Sure I am functioning in such a way
That my decisions and my life
Are mine.

12/23/04

Let us not talk
Of such dismal things.
Instead, let us
Embrace the newfound life
Prominent within us
Each day.
The miraculous glow
That envelops us inside
And shows so far
Past our exteriors,
Enough to make us cry out
And proclaim that we are alive!

12/23/04

In the Silence

In the silence, I no longer hear,
And I also find that
I can no longer see.
(Can no one explain) what
Has come over me?
In the silence, brooding, I sit,
While this veil hangs over my eyes
And causes me to comprise thoughts
That shall never reach the public domain.
Do I even have a name?
Such a concept is so foreign to me
Because this has only let things be
Any way but the way that
I would like it!
Now comes the time where
I must allow all this emotion
To fade to black.

12/23/04

Rimbaud?
No, too mild of an association for you.
Such a genius, such a bright perspective
You have on a life so foreign to you—
A life that you should be able to someday lead!
Stand tall, young brother,
Now knowing that you can, oh, stand and embrace
The world as a man!
Proud legs take their first steps to the life,
Which God has given him from the miracle worker,
Who has delivered you from a desperate state.
And I, for one, am proud to have this opportunity to
Listen vicariously to your profound words,
Printed neatly on each page.
A nation's heart you have touched, beating
So proudly in the body of our world.

12/23/04

Covet

Comfort in touching
The pillow that calls my name
Is nothing compared to
Pushing myself to the limit—
Hours without sleep or food;
Sometimes, it perplexes me
As to why mortals need both.
Oh, freedom lies only forty winks away,
But I must keep myself at bay long enough
To at least carry out an inkling of a thought.
There! Now I may please retreat to this other world
Often visited by my mind?
I am in need of its great comfort right now.

12/23/04

These extra inches,
How am I going to
Shed them so my
Inner being can shine?
Chalking my body full of
Healthy food and stretching myself
To flatten the cells.
(I’ve lost) just enough
To keep up my false hope—
Enough to have me wishing
I had the potential to
Do it all!
And I have yet to feel the
Full splendor, but I hope
It’s not too far from my grasp
Because the world cannot
Be put on hold.

12/23/04

My eyes let you see into my world,
But they will cast you out if you are
Not careful—if they detect any potential discomfort.
What do you want, why do you so desperately
What to delve into my life?
It makes me believe that something is missing
From yours, and I don't know if I can provide
What you need.
You claim that you know what you need,
But you can only see your face in the blue reflection
Of dreams, but you think that I am, somehow,
The answer to your prayers and the dreams you
Have hidden in your head, though I don't even know
What I want for my life—you haven't even
Assigned any priorities, suffice to say, you have
Embarked upon this all too soon.

12/23/04

Back to the same place,
And I don't know what to do
In a feeling so long rewarded.
Yes, we have found an
Accumulation of thoughts
Gathered in my mind;
But no one can decipher them.
So much to know,
I have no space left to speak
Because nothing else can be found.

12/24/04

Marks a thought close to catastrophe,
When all the morals and values finally
Come sinking in.
But it's too late.
What has been wasted time before
Should have gone to instill these things
Into many heads.
As much as I would like to admit
That I have the power to turn back time,
I cannot.
As much as I can rid the world of their errs,
I must admit that comes with the human territory.
Oh, these lamentations are pointless
Because nothing can be done of my accord;
I have nothing to do with the divinity
That descends to earth on a daily basis.
Alas, all their time here is through;
We must not acknowledge their presence
In the afterlife and know that they
Have finally reached their salvation.

12/24/04

Write on demand,
I am going to deny
These false accusations,
Even though boredom
Gnaws at my brain
And tears mercilessly
At every part of it
As I try to hide all the
Misleading evidence.

12/23/04

I miss the beautiful warmth
Of which you complain—sun
Rolling as the clouds stream
Across the sky.
How long did you plan on
Playing the part of the recluse?
I can just see your body
As it's draped across your bed
And your sad spirit sinking
Further into your chest; the world
Cannot just go away.

12/23/04

Method to the madness,
That's inherent in our lives.
Why do such things happen,
And how do we let the world
Know it's about due
For a change?
So many have yet to open their ears
And their minds to be attune—
So they are not dull with ignorance,
That likes to consume us whole
When we least expect it.
Oh, to err no more, to change
Our existence to the ideal,
But what is ideal, anyway?

12/23/04

I hear the dismayed cries
Of the people who can
Relate most to pain—
They who feel the
Only possibilities
Come from harm or removing
Themselves from this world
(That they feel) holds no promise.
If only things could change…

12/23/04

Kindred Spirit

To get into the mind of the man,
Who has brought me so much thought,
So much inspiration.
I wish I could say that he
Sang songs of jubilance,
But his life makes me sad
To a point, but I might be better
For having this opportunity to know—
To explore, and to relate to
This spectacular human being,
Who should have been spared
All this heartache.
My soul feels for you.

*dedicated to Elliott Smith

12/23/04

The shallow world,
Of which I sometimes
Strive to enter, has me
Captivated with its
Undertones of negativity—
The same things that
Many tend to overlook.
All the glitter that floats
On the surface hides
Whatever unpleasantries of
This alleged perfect ideal.
They cannot fool the likes of people—
Those who house thought in their minds
On a regular basis.

12/23/04

Into the arms of some loving
Human being.
I suppose that is what
Everyone needs, whether
Their exteriors allow them
To know this or not.
Oh, the things that other people
Allow themselves to see—
Some think that they can burn a hole
Right through me, but they
Will soon find they cannot get
What they want that way.
Love, yes, comes in many forms,
But it is up to the individual
To find these things within themselves—
To take the first step before anyone
Braves the storm into your heart.

12/23/04

Lean strings, watch the man,
As he stands so tall and takes
It upon himself to block the sunlight for all.
To a small child sitting below,
He may seem (to be) the greatest
Figure of all.
In such delicate, impressionable eyes,
The world can seem to be a great
Place of innocence—
Comparable to Blake.
Watching the white
Clouds soaring above
His head, even though they seem to
Be touching the tips of his hair
Spirited laughter at a silly face,
Like from an individual in a movie.
Such a pity to know that these feelings
Will wear off as time progresses,
But I suppose it would be a crime
To disillusion the youth while
Still barely emerged from its seed—
Just getting a first taste of sunlight,

Filtered through the

Head of its protector.

12/23/04

When I hear the song
That crushes the spirit of those
Who feel they have already
Lost the last remnants of the sanity,
I know that something sinister has
Been enforced by man.
Do others dare not grow suspicious
Of what they see and hear?

12/23/04

Weep, just as the last cherubs
Put on the face of this planet.
They should have something
Left inside them that links them
To their heavenly realm.
Oh, and they should know from
Whence they came to ease the pangs
Of this earth and the sadness that can
Come from a broken heart.
Words of wisdom from an elder,
Who has at least some compassion
To form such thoughts—yes, I can do
My bit for those who need guidance
In this menagerie of madness.

12/23/04

You embody so much—so many
Good qualities known by those
Who hold you dear in life.
People could take lessons from your
Compassion—learn from observation
And the great love that comes
From God.
Not so many I know have these
Qualities (that should be) essential
In the making of man, so it is from
My humble heart that I give thanks,
In hopes that there is something I can do
To repay every precious favor.

12/23/04

In each lifetime, everyone has someone
With whom they can identify and can know
They are loved.
In each lifetime, everyone should feel
The joy from hearts who prioritize,
Thus showing forth the component
That should rule the world, should deliver
Man from his sin.
Oh, the Lord has seen me safely blessed,
And He shall not forget those who have
Renewed my energy and happiness in life.
And, every night, these lips, hands, and heart
Pray that you shall receive all the finest blessings
On earth and that the heavens reserve
A glorious spot for those who have touched
The lives of someone, who could not do
Some good in return.
A fine tale of heavenly love from which
Everyone should learn and can gain
Inspiration for their lives.

12/28/04

It appears if I am at a loss
For words—all that I have said
Has been dragged into my mind,
But let me just say out of my poor
Fatigue, thank God for you
And all that you do.
Oh, without your sweet salvation,
I would be lost amidst this life, never to see
Another smiling face—never to fall into another,
Sweet embrace.

12/28/04

Let us see what this has to offer—
How this is to bring about some change.
This reminds me of those people
Who are climbing to the light
And ascending to higher ground.
They are unafraid because they know
That no peril lies ahead in the splendid
Journey of incredible faith.

12/29/04

~~~~~~

Fill my heart
With the undying joy,
For which it has longed
So many years, as I have tried
To find a passage in the making.

12/29/04
~~~~~~

The sound is so pristine
That it hardly seems real.
As for its intent, I suppose
That it is meant to give people
The impression of an angelic flight
As they find peace and tranquility
Within themselves.
Now is the time.

12/29/04

For those who have
Missed the overtones,
Of similar music and a
Climbing façade, feel
Inclined to know that my message
Does not mean sorrow, as the
Fingers hit the minor keys.
Rather, be glad that one can see
A fire burning within us all,
As it points out the beauty
Inherent in this life.

12/29/04

Listen, as I say
That all should be well—
In the changing over
Of the worlds, as we
Are delivered from our
Residence to the ideal.

12/29/04

This has always
Held such a special place
In my heart of hearts.
Why, this is something
To which many modern man
Can relate!
In this, I have found another
Part of my youth
That shan't die, as long as
My memory serves me.
Those days when I lived to
Set the world on fire,
The epitome of my youth!

12/19/04

Something stirs inside me
And makes me feel that
I must appreciate, or at least
Pay homage to something
So unfamiliar,
As so many different versions
Run through my head.
Having said enough said,
I must move on to a
New platform…

12/29/04

What will I do
When words fail to come at me
For a time?
Could you ease the suffering,
And would you know of
The cruelties of this isolation—
The very desolation that has
Resulted from the sieve of my mind?
Then, you must know that most of my
Enthusiasm has already gone.

12/29/04

Play for me anything,
Besides the dreadful melancholy
That has taken root in my mind.
In the ballroom, they dance,
With all the emotion wiped
Clear from their faces, and
No curtains have been drawn
To show in the light.
None of this can be right,
Wrong in every corner.

12/29/04

Their kind gifts

Have fulfilled my body,

Spirit, and mind.

They have given me

A piece of my mind,

They have represented

A great love passed on by the

Finest of humankind.

And, for that, they should

Take great pride.

12/19/04

Why so downtrodden?
You have just been given
Something that will help you
Regain the bounce in your step—
Something that has already taken
The initiative for you in entering
This new world.

12/29/04

Offers to give
And let others feel
The merriment
Abundant in the vibrant
Souls, who wake the world
With their resounding cries,
As to let them know that
It is time for them to rise
And greet each new day,
Just as intended by God.

12/29/04

The same night,
Every year, comes
To remind humankind
How each and every soul
Is blessed with the gift of
Eternal love.
Oh, how we need to be
Reminded, sometimes, of
Our births.
This has allowed so many
To see the light!

12/29/04

My heels kicked up
In the air, as I dance
To the planned choreography
In the streets, although
Life is no dress rehearsal.
Now that we’ve got everything
Down pat, we can take a look
At where we sat.

12/29/04

For all of you I pray,
Right now, and before
My head hit the pillow
Last night.
I prayed for
All the victims
Who were
Forced to departure—
Their earthly vessels behind
Upon their untimely leave.
Oh, this wretched disaster,
I can only say that I hope
These people are at their
New destinations, though
They left at too short a time!
Right now, I can
Find no reason
Or rhyme as
To why all this
Has occurred
But, rest assured,
They have made their

Way to eternal peace,

Even though

So many have wanted them

To remain behind, but their souls,

In memory, shall not be erased.

*dedicated to the tsunami victims of December 26, 2004

12/29/04

Do you know how it feels to be tied down,
So physically and mentally exhausted that you
Feel every substance drain—so weak that
You feel the chains cutting into your skin
From a muscle collapse?
And it makes me wonder how I could have
Allowed myself to become this way when my
Only cure is sleep.
All the time, I seem to be getting in too deep.
Alas! I cannot move to even bang my head
In frustration.

12/19/04

As I slowly slip for your grasp,
I close my eyes right before
I fall to the floor.
Then, your footsteps chase my
Shadowy remnants through
The corridor, but nothing remains.
“I am not good enough!” I cry,
As I have completely dissolved
All meaning.

12/29/04

Age, Oh No!

Up late, reading a book,
Although most of this has
Been brought to mind before.
Ms. Angelou has reason to be proud,
For she has conquered so much.
Though, here comes the questions of age,
To which she has graciously answered.
And, now, I can see them all, fading
Beauties hiding behind written word;
I shall not become one of them!
Now I make sure that my frame
Remains small and my legs can kick,
Walk, and stretch just as hard and high.
Brown hair still long and beautiful,
As my skin remains ever firm—
Enough so to convince many
That I seem so many years younger.
Ah, my poor brain shall not be left
Out as (it will) be nourished
By the very substances that keep my

Body alive, though some may

Still question my sanity—

So little a price

To pay to have the rest

Of these things remain firm!

1/2/05

My Truest Love

The many times I tried to leave,
I found I could not.
I found I had to stay someone who could always
Make me feel confident and warm
In my creations and alterations.
Others have hardly given me a fair chance;
They would always try to humble a poor soul
That needed no humility, and they made me feel
That my advances are less than worthy.
Humiliation and frustration;
The world would never know me through them
Because they have not remarked on your splendid creation.
Yes, a great part of me has been fulfilled
Through being able to measure my life's worth,
And mankind will know how much I have fallen in love
With the words that have enabled me to
Produce my greatest works.

1/2/05

My sweet little face
Hides in the corner,
Projects a pensive frown,
As if to say, "Let me out
Of this place."
I can see that all the others
Feel the same.
What was he thinking
By brining us to a stadium?
We, the art students who
Could care less about sports.
Now all that has changed for me,
But I choose not to root for my hometown.
When asked why, I just smile
And say that my reservations are
Held for others.
And, you can see that was true,
But I liked no football team
During my younger days.

1/2/05

In a restaurant with these other girls.
I know them; I could recognize their faces.
But, the one across from me—she and I
Really got on well, and I wonder what
She is up to these days.
(What would she think, knowing that I
Inquire about her all the time?)
Some things may please her, while others
May shock, jogged for her to remember
That I exist and was a minor part of her life.
Perhaps she would note that I moved on a little,
While she moved on a lot
(With her and others I am).
Stuck in a different world, though we are cut
From the same cloth.
So many people are.

1/3/05

Through the laughter of others,
I am hidden, as if something embarrassing
Has taken over the moment.
One can see an inkling of a smile on my face,
Which leads me to believe that I was a person
Trying to fit into the crowd.
Back in those days, I tried many things
To amuse others, but then a part of me
Is hiding from the type of thing
This world might want me to be,
What these others see as a capability would
Cause us to live conflicting lives
If we would have to be together
Out of our pretense.
And, years from now, we can see all the
Changes that have taken place since then,
But I am glad to say that I've changed
For the better because I have stuck
To my beliefs.

1/3/05

What look has crossed my face,
As I have just been caught in the lens;
Did the sun get in my eyes?
I look like a portrait of the complacency
Of youth, so easily disturbed by the wrong moves,
And so uncaring of what some people think.
Was I contemplating my future,
Or maintaining certain qualities of my youth?
Clearly, I wanted to look away from the
Others' examples, maybe that still remains true today.
No matter what you say, I like the picture all the same.

1/4/05

My height makes me feel
As if I am towering over my comrades,
Who seem to be a little more focused,
Eyes so distant from the camera lens.
Neck muscles stretch to lift my head
In the air, where I can feel an oncoming
Air of superiority.
Had it ever occurred to me, then, to
Form my perception for the future?
Did I think that I would be looking at this,
Years from now, while trying to
Define my life?
Could be.

1/4/05

In the background, next to the speaker
Who heard that things were going downhill
For me. Unfortunately, I did not have the
Opportunity to tell him that things are better.
This makes me wonder where he is right now.
Such memories from those times, you can
See the inherent boredom on our faces,
But worries laid heavy on my mind at that time,
As, sometimes, they do today.
   Funny how a part of me has changed
To take the physical, as well as the mental;
He may not even recognize me today.

1/5/05

Before I rest my weary head—
Before my eyes close to give me tranquility,
I need some kind of stability to ensure
The rest of my life.
What shall I do, oh, where should I go?
I wish all these demons could be released
From my head as I try to find a solid purpose
For my life.
[Others have already done the same.]
I never thought this day would have arrived,
But it has; I never thought these choices
Would be mine, but they are.
And I have this to worry about in the
Midst of the confusion because something
In my mind is preventing me from thinking
Properly; this should not have to be an obstacle!
When I was younger, what a tragedy that would be,
But, now, I have to make more with larger responsibility.
Adding on the stress, I can't think about this right now
Because I need some rest.

1/5/05

Day 2

Suspension of belief,
Will I really be as tired
As people make me out to be?
I hope that I can maintain
A healthy attitude—sanity
People may not quite know how
To perceive me, but all that's
Unimportant is put on
The back burner for now,
So at least I can pretend.

1/4/05

Feet standing still on the earth,

Who knows how long (I have)

Until I am buried alive in the tomb of ambiguity?

Sweat slowly trickles down my neck

As he walks through the door.

1/4/05

The next closest thing to rapture
Cannot be mine until
I have the guts to decide something—
Anything that would ensure
Some stability.
My feet bounce on the floorboards
To match the state of my mind,
Constantly in motion.
Some part of me still thinks
That I have more time to
Decide these things.

1/4/05

There goes that thought,
Rushing back into my head—
The same ugly thought that
Devoured me nearly three years ago,
But my poor heart fears it can
Only be worse this time.
Lord knows that I have tried to
Do my best—learn from my past.
Alas! I cannot always change the world.
That would require a supernatural strength,
Impossible for my status—then my face
Makes the color of the purest snow
That falls from the heavens.

1/4/05

Narrow strips of identification,
You expect me to be as slender
As the next small thing,
Talk about an oxymoron.
Yes, there were days when the
Shallow thinking never stuck,
But times have changed, and
I am shying away from old age;
Funny how I eventually changed my mind,
Just so long as I can keep my previous values,
The best of both worlds!

1/4/05

You can feel the bones in my lower arm
As you try to reach out and save me
From being devoured alive—emaciated
Living in its personification.
Once, I lost track, then I woke up
In a terrifying reality that I may be
The doom of me.
Bag of bones, knocking on your door.

1/4/05

~~~~~~

As I sleep, my body shudders,
As my soul leaves it for a time—
Having it open for invaders,
For the ambiguities that are my dreams.
Sometimes, my mind is pleased.
Others, it recoils, depending on
What I was thinking the previous day.

1/4/05
~~~~~~

Overturn from two weeks—
I feel as I have lost every ounce
Of human dignity I ever had.
Stuffed suits stare down my
Tiny profile as it begins to
Shake in trepidation.

1/4/05

Paradise Found

At long last, I have managed
To find an earthly utopia—
A place almost equal to a
Heavenly realm.
The only tears that are
Allowed to escape from my
Eyes of those of joy when
I cry in exaltation!
And every light footstep walks
Across the sky, as my light
Body enjoys the winds warm
Embrace.
I must never leave this
Place, my haven,
 Paradise found!

1/4/05

Three men at the bar,
The key to a trinity—
The butcher, the baker,
And the candlestick maker
Of modern day.
People appreciate trade
As they admire their suits,
Their great importance.

1/4/05

Oh, I lied, I must cry;
I must allow me to grieve my situation.
This unsure feeling, my sixth sense perceives
That something is wrong.
It came at the most inappropriate time
Of my life, when I have yet to establish
My name.
I mourn for our love, will it ever be the same?
Bless his warm heart, which contrasts
With my strong mind; bless my open lines
Of communication.
An epiphany—something happened
Last night when I collapsed into his arms.
I wanted to cry, I am so uncertain of my feelings
At the time.
Would I be letting go of the last thing
That I ever had—how can both your hearts heal?
Sometimes, I think we're the glue that holds
Each other together.
His cool emotional sense
And my physical pride—the flair to my temper
And the gateway to his health; I used to

Operate on stealth!
Pounce on the unsuspecting victims, as they
Showed a remote interest in me, and I watched it
Build up until I wanted to stop; I have no idea!
Just the mere thought has crossed my mind
Many a time, but I should not act upon it quite yet.

1/4/05

Mental torture and conscious state;
I am unconscious most of the time.
Haunted when I sleep, burdened
While I am awake.
Just a ghost of me survives;
I feel like the poor *artist,
Living in nineteenth century
Spain, what was his name?
It's amazing how he allowed himself
To sleep in such a tortured state,
In any human condition.
Don't let this happen to a youth such as I!
No fame, perhaps infamy, of which to speak;
I have enough to go on a small level.

*dedicated to Francesco Goya

1/4/05

Women (what kind)?
Do you prefer the type
Who crawl all over you,
Using their aesthetic charm,
Flinging hands, legs, and breasts
All over the parts of your body?
I should like to think that
You fancy the silent type,
A little less self-assured.
(I would ask, only I am far too shy
To make my way over to your corner.)
You can only imagine what
I have stored in my mind,
But you know what is running through
Her transparent brain.
The suspense is driving me insane!

1/4/05

Curious eyes,

Looking over my works,

My life—they are a true gift

From God, far more

Worth than any human progeny

That would spring right from me!

(I have) over five-thousand,

Created by my human mind

And written by my hands.

1/4/05

Hidden in the alcove
Where hardly anyone, if anybody
Can see me.
Later in the day,
I like it that way!
Just my means of hanging a sign:
DO NOT DISTURB, to ward off
Any offenders.
They all should have gotten
The message by now.

1/4/05

Pressure building up inside,
How much can I take before
I explode?
People who tried to steer me right
Only wanted to me to feel my delight
And the conquering of my fears.
How can I survive the
Tuning of the years?
Auch du, I knew, I had the feeling
That this was going to be hard—
That it would take all my concentration,
Until I am completely drained.
Either way, I have to make it through
The day so that no one will have
Anything negative to say.

1/5/05

Yet again, I am here, prone to mediocrity
For the time.
Sometimes, I wonder if my life
If going to open up and lead me
To a safe haven—a stable place
In which I will be able to reap my rewards.
God knows I've had proper guidance,
God knows I can keep myself under control—
I have been able to hold things in before.
Certain times, I don't know if I have
Enough of anything so that I can
Live comfortably; I don't want to be
One of the tragic work stories.
One part of me likes this exploitation,
But I know nothing else!

1/5/05

My skin the color of purity,
And my eyes project a vacant stare.
People trying to come through
In so many different directions—
Trying to ask me if something is wrong.
They do not know what has happened,
And I am hardly aware of my existence.
Might this be a case of ignorance is bliss
Because I feel no pain, only shock that has
Sent me into outer space.
(I can feel) anxious hands place themselves
On my arm as they lead me from this room
To another; I've no idea where I'm really going.

1/5/05

Drowning in a pool of self-pity and self-hate.
I can't; I refuse to believe that something like this
Could happen to me!
Precautions taunting me over my head,
But they should not embark on this victory.
Dance when they have failed, I've failed.
God, where is the humanity I once found within myself,
In the splendid account of mankind?
No, faith is not lost, even though worry
Has settled in, taking over the recesses
Of my addled brain.
I know not what to think, hoping for the best
In my prayers!

1/5/05

You are not welcome, no one
Is welcome inside me!
I have a life of my own,
A soul of my own and, every night,
I pray to God that I am alone
Before I fall asleep—before I trek
To each new day; why should I be
Further tormented?
I am here, after all, which should be
Enough torture to last until I reach
The next phase, is there any way I can
Relieve these days so I could have
Found myself a future that involves
No one but myself until I get a good start?

1/6/05

You see the circles under my eyes,
The luminous circles that contrast
With the whiteness of my face.
Hear the gentle tone of my voice,
Trying to keep me out of trouble.
Back away, back away from the people,
Who conflict with my life and try to
Put me down for my decisions.
Alone, God knows that I would like
To be alone in my bed and safe
From the troubles of the world—
My hands resigned
To portraying the turmoil
That currently envelops my soul.
I am losing control,
Help me get through
This alleged tragedy, let the world see me
As a decent human being!
Most everyone suffers from fear
Of the unknown, suffice to say, they fear me
As well.
They've no need to.

Life offers so many choices,

And I would prefer

To believe that I worship a merciful God.

What is selfish without the word "self," anyway?

Stop forcing all your old ideas into my head!

1/6/05

My God, it has happened again—
No surprise, for this occurrence
Is where I lost my words, the lost thoughts
In my mind.
When this happens, sometimes, I feel
I have lost my worth as a human being
Because I cannot portray the agony and
The ecstasy of life—love and strife involve
A kind of inspiration that makes me
Regain all my magnificent power
In the finest hour.

1/6/05

A gentle kiss from the
Warm rays of the sun.
Welcome!
Welcome back after your
Three-day absence.
Clouds poured down misery in your place
And soured the moods of so many.
Please stay, if even only for a little while,
To brighten the moods of men who
Doubted that you would return for days.
Now they do not have to believe their words
Because their misery has stopped long enough
For us to rejoice.

1/6/05

Fear of expressing, as thought
That it may not come true.
I do not want to say, and I
Only know that I am thinking
If a person in this world
Knew my thoughts, they may
Question, but why should I
Care because they are not me?
And, I am not them, but
These mixed thoughts should
Go unsaid for now.

1/6/05

I felt so pretty, pretty enough
To think I was the queen of the world,
Or at least a small region of it.
Seated on my high horse,
Thinking I could ride any stallion.
But it turns out that I have no reason
To celebrate because I deserve nothing—
Lowered myself to a point that
I swore I would never do; if it's
All the same to you, I think I'll
Hide in the darkest corner, away from
The human contact that would surely trouble me.
I can almost feel him coming this way,
But he does not know his presence is
Not welcome.
His mind does not know my thoughts—
It's not connected to mine, perhaps
He won't see me at all.

1/7/05

As touching as the moment, I don’t think
We could fare well together and make a life
For ourselves, unless some changes are made,
According to meet the needs.
You went in and smoothed the way
Until I decided to join, so it’s needless to
Remind you how you went in, knowing
What I said did not ever want and, now, I have to
Remind you almost every time we meet.
This is certainly not a good sign!
So many other things should be on my mind,
And here it remains stuck on you.
Do you think very often about me?
I know you have these thoughts floating around
Inside your head, and you may not know
How to get them out.
I suppose I could help you, either help,
Or walk out on the picture, which I do not want to do.
Just tell me in a dream if you want all this
To go through the way things are planned.

1/9/05

Here when I should have thought
Of something to keep me afloat.
I need some force to move me
Out of my backup plan so I can
Spread my wings and slowly do
The best that I can.
I suppose that not all these things
Are going to go along smoothly—
Only when I'm ready.

1/10/05

The same tunes, blasting
Through my ears nearly every day,
Causes me to forget my inspiration.
And, one day, I'll wake up in
A helpless stupor and wonder
Where it all went.
My favorite argument always
Comes into play when people say
That I've used it all up when I was young.
And my pretty head was full of new ideas;
Why can't it be that way again?

1/19/05

I must maintain that I am trying
To achieve the status of an
Independent woman.
Oh, I am in need of help, even though
I've come a long way so, every night,
I pray to find my niche in this life—
Pray that all my talents be put to good use
In bed at night, clutching my pillow
With anticipation, as if I am clinging
Onto a dream that would either defy,
Or define, my life, which has dragged
Me into its realm.
When I was younger, I had the standard plan
In mind, but I have done so much more
Than some would have thought possible.

1/10/05

This disgusts me, just thinking
That I could let myself go in
This hideous direction at your
Discretion w/ my cynicism,
(That's a terrible word to use).
But I know how some people
Categorize those who like to
Take a stand.

1/10/05

Other women, listen!

Gloria Steinem, I have

Stirred up a bit of controversy

In my day, and I enjoy

Being able to see the beautiful woman

You've become.

And I should hope that I can

Become her, too, with my

Childfree womb and my aged soul.

This healthy body will look back

And have to be repulsed by nothing.

1/10/05

Something in the air
Does not want me to move—
No stirring from this spot, these
Comfortable thoughts that
I'm supposed to think
Right now
Are too taboo, as an unknown identity
Runs through my skin, chilling my bones.
These things happen, and I wish I could
Take them back into my arms and
Ease their pain because all this would
Take nations of help and consolation.
Right now, my sorrow shall not
Be expressed through written word
Because this fear is holding me back.

1/10/05

How sad it is when I am
Reduced to “settling down” and
“Acting my age” by those
Who think they have all the
Say in the world.
Age will not see my physical degradation;
Age will not quench my mental fires!
I’ll still have rosy cheeks
And youth’s passionate desire.
The Romantics would be pleased;
Those who knew me back then
Would not be surprised to know
That I have not changed for the worse.
Ah, I can only get better, thus knowing
That the sweet taste of victory will
Always be on my tongue.

1/10/05

They've got good hearts, but the bitter
Eyes inside my head cannot see how
They can relate to common man
With all their fine riches, unless they
Think of a past life.
Family history, I should think
They would also like to care
For their loved ones.
Now all that is possible for them,
They should see no need for worry,
Knowing that their loved ones will
Have the best of care.
Every day, I dare to have these thoughts,
But I cannot help myself right now!

1/10/05

Thoughts of love, thoughts of
Uncertainty all formulating
In my head as
I call his image to mind.
I want to see him, but I don't know
If I want his company.
Yet I am hiding inside myself—
Inside of a shadow of the girl
Who I used to be.
What kind of a façade must
I put on as I pretend to look forward
To the future—
The nights that took place
In the past are a vague memory
Inside my head.
These differences jutting
Out of my mind; where do we
Go from here?
Life has made us both so different,
But we both went in,
Hoping for the best,
But the best cannot happen until we

Both know what we want.

Some things have no compromise.

1/10/05

My portly hips thrashing as I walk,
Hoping to get money, hoping to
Lose a little weight—thus taking up less space.
You know I get frustrated when my
Metabolism slows, and I hit a plateau.
I feel like I have been fighting this
Battle for years, but this is such a small
Amount of time in the grand scheme of things.
Support, I need endless support to
Keep up this harrowing task,
This thing that occupies my mind
Three forth of the time.
Years from now, I must be able
To look back and say that I have been
Healthy, perfectly trim—to win the hearts
Of men at least twenty years younger
And beat them in almost every category,
All because I knew how to keep myself alive.

1/10/05

You were so beautiful; the words
That you have read, so far,
Have led me to believe that
I actually knew you—that
You were a great part of my life,
In the flesh.
You were someone that I supported
And rooted for all throughout
Your obstacles; I know that you have
Helped me during these parts of my life
That made me think things are difficult.
Please tell me that things are all right
And peace has become everything
In your afterlife.
At night, I can hear you, the music
Speaks through your voice, and a
Supporting hand is placed on my shoulder.
When a certain part of me numbs,
And I know that you are around—
You will be where you are when
I come to the heavens and greet you
With gladness in knowing that God has

Provided you with great comfort.
That may have not been
Abundant in this life
Rest in peace, my darling muse,
Until we can meet…

*dedicated to Elliott Smith

1/12/05

~~~~~~

Compared to the ominous skies outside,
We look warm and inviting, but is that
Always the case?
That's not true all the time with our souls.

1/11/05
~~~~~~

Just thinking about things today
Makes me feel on edge—
My feet not even planted
Firmly on the ground.
One small, frightening noise
Is enough to send me in flight,
And I don't even have to listen
To the voices in my head.
Sometimes, I wonder about my
Tangible being and if I am only
A product of divine intervention.
Instead, I may well have been
A being of eternal design,
Hovering over those
Unsuspecting of me
Coming into their lives.
What divine creatures have been sent
To keep a watch over me?
Some kind of darkness
Threatens me,
Unnerves my poor body to the point that
Ghosts make me want to hide—

Somewhere that I will not be bothered.
Though warm, my body tingles, and the
Small lumps on my flesh remain
Touched by the wind, as my body shakes,
Because someone is walking over my grave.
I don't quite know what's going on,
But I know I've had enough, I know
That I want to go back to my earthly home
And barricade myself in solitude, until people
Think of me as a ghost.
Then, I will come out of my bewilderment
Because all this will make sense, and I will
Have to fear no more; fear no more these things
That were previously unknown.

1/13/05

Just let me move, given an opportunity
To blow off some steam.
A bit of small exercise will help me
Keep my cool.
Anger made me small, but the
"Noxious fumes" grew me to a size
That even the harshest of bullies
Would have to flee in trepidation.
Just as long this keeps up
So that I can maintain the stability
That ensures everyone's good will.

1/13/05

Great indentations,
My sides are now concave,
And I feel that the good changes
Have already taken place,
As my bones are protruding
Through my skin.
Those who accredit my actions
With extreme obsession have
Much to learn because some
Of my mentality may do them good!

1/13/05

Lying through my teeth,
While trying to keep with those
Who would eagerly tear off my head.
What is I don't like the local colors
(Or regional realism)?
To each different tastes, let me
Be free to dislike what I choose,
And I'll understand this infatuation
You have with the local team,
Who is overplayed in my mind.

1/13/05

Damn it all
For having to be here,
Or anywhere, that makes
My mood sour.
How degrading, the things
They make us do for the public,
Who hardly appreciates them at all.
I don’t want to be near these people,
Unless they offer me more for
My valuable time because I should
Be off, making my mark on the world.

11/13/05

I'd hate to think that bad dreams
Could be the source of what
Plagues your head
As you drive in your car,
Even for a brief second.
Just let the lingering smoke
Fly over your head, as you
Think about what he might have left.
One thing, the tingling in your hand
When you used to place it on his arm—
Nothing can do you any harm
While you're sleeping side by side.
Now the empty space in your bed
Unnerves you to the point that you
Hold your breath, in hopes
Of staying awake because these dreams
Only break your peace of mind,
Whatever little is left.

11/13/05

I know my gut told me,
But I already know that all.
The animosity is coming back!
I had to figure, part of me
Felt an urge to pump it
Out into the crowd.
Testosterone—do you usually
Associate smoldering anger
With males, even though
I can be more dangerous than
Many that I know?
There is no such thing as perfection,
No one can hold a calm temper all the time.
And the crowd can see the steam flow
Through my ears, and my face looks
As though it's been burned by the sun,
Only there is no sun, and they can
See right through my false front.
Who would have thought that
All this would come back so soon?

1/13/05

Proud,

But hesitant.

I would like to believe

That you can do it—

Clear away the obstacles

That plagued you before.

These things that held you down

Will be blown out of here

And thrown into kingdom come.

Prepare me to march in your army,

And I will stand by you, wearing your colors

With pride as you take down the black

And gold with everything that you have.

Just say the word, and I will be by your side—

Helping you achieve what

Should be yours after all you have been through.

Perseverance on your side will see you

Through again, as your fight for the title once more.

*dedicated to the New England Patriots

1/17/05

Why did I do it again?
How could I let him;
How could I allow
Myself (to be)
Dragged through the
Digestive mire—
Poisoning my only body, thus
Allowing my fat to protrude?
They do this all the time,
But they don’t
Even seem to care
Souls screaming out, “Oh, help!”
While bodies are firmly seated
On the chair, looking for the
Next virtual target to kill.
(At least their minds still
Work to form strategies for
Their digital paradise.)
I can’t live like them; I have
To let myself get up and
Do the things my poor body
Has needed me to for

Quite some time.

What it now wants me to do,

Thanks to a little

Thing called devotion—

Motivation to keep me at my peak form.

1/17/05

All well and good for you
To cut down things I enjoy—
The things I hold closest to my heart.
And my response can only
Encourage to continue this—
The defamation of their names.
Don't you think, that sometimes,
Your insults go beyond the surface
And cut into my very soul?
You say I should lighten up,
But I know that I could fling some words
In your direction that may make you
Feel like less of a man—less of a
Human being.
Don't make fun of the way I cry
Because tears could fall from your eyes,
The tears lamenting the loss of me—
(One of the best things you've ever had)
If all this ridicule
Does not come to a stop!

1/17/05

The corporates are all in.
Now they think I have to do
What they say, as if my career
Is hinging on a string.
Well, I’ve got news for you;
It’s not!
These people think they have
Done me the greatest service,
But my mind has much
Room to complain.
So listen accordingly
When I speak of my education—
The thing that has gained me
Part of my worth.
Explain the sequences that made me
A part of your team—
A cog in some
Shoddy assembly line that claims its
Value is higher than it really is.
Some part of me should
Be ashamed, but another part
Knows I have to keep on going

So that I may not become destitute,

Despite my situation.

You may not know what I mean,

But you'd better treat me

Like a human being!

1/17/05

Too quiet, I can barely hear
Your beautiful noise as it
Comes into my ears.
Turn it up, allow it to sink
Into my mind as your life's
Intensity is presented to me yet again.
Oh, all this makes more sense
Now that I got to read the story of your life.
People today must be set straight
On the records, things that prove
Your existence to a generation
Of new listeners.
They need to know the truth.

*dedicated to Elliott Smith (113-126)

1/20/05

The beautiful strumming of a guitar,
As it related to the fantasies
Of your mind.
I can relate about wanting to
Get away from the everyday crowd.
Who are you going to take with you?

1/20/05

Times have changed since even
The most recent days, even though
Your sound tends to remain the same—
Recorded for my pleasure or misery,
Whichever happens to come around
At the moment.
I am used to the bittersweet tones
That you have to offer, that you
Seem to want the whole world to hear
Awake! Time and time again
To know that you are there,
In my possession, whenever my psyche
Needs to know how to deal with—
Whatever is presented at any given time.

1/20/05

What has happened to the poor person
Of which you speak?
 Sweet love, sweet girl, who you
Held so dear.
Times have taken her away
From her heritage and into the danger,
Although it was not deliberate on your part.
Nothing ever was, according to your "allies,"
Those friends who have turned tail
Then done you wrong.
Such a shame, living in the midst of
A modern tragedy.

1/20/05

You had to turn
To these things
To put back the pieces
Of your life that
Have fallen out of
Your control.
At the time, I know
Friends have tried to
Help whenever they can,
But nothing seemed to
Get through without
A bottle marked with an
Rx. Oh, how
Sad but true;
We tried to save you.

1/20/05

Part of you must have known—
An intuition given to animals
Before they die.
The whole world wants to know
To whom you are referring
When you mention this friend—
Addressed to people who could
Have made a difference.
Could we have betrayed you,
Unknowingly?
Lord knows so many wanted
Your well-being, including
Those whom you've never met.

1/20/05

The cold superficialities of the world;
I know that you did not like them
Because they tried to drag you in.
Your friends were also no stranger
To the crime.
It's a shame that these things happened,
But so many got to know you
Through the small amount of fame
You achieved in this world that has
Also done you wrong.
(Such an) angel with broken wings;
Who could point out your fate?

1/20/05

Some of the girls who you have loved
Still lie awake during the nights
When you are most on their mind.
Fans, away from conventionality,
Who had issues within themselves,
Sometimes cry at your picture,
Hanging in their minds.
They wish this song was for them,
Even though they never
Knew your situation—
Crickets chirp at night.

1/20/05

Parallel to popular belief
Is the fear of failure and
The unaccepting minds of those
Who could never understand
Your genius.
There are many of those, but some
Still know what you have done
And how far you could have come.

1/20/05

~~~~~~

What part of you still feels so tiny,
As to fit through these intentions,
Without having the repercussions
Of anyone noticing the slightest
Hint of your existence?
It may be very difficult, but some part
Will always come through for you.

1/20/05
~~~~~~

Scorn over some woman's behavior,
Someone you could have had.
Who knows what you were really thinking
When you saw them from across the room?
Quoting some memory from the past,
Degradation of the girl who you
Thought you knew.
She couldn't handle your brains,
So she settled for someone who could never
Be your intellectual equal—a thing that
People do when they have no other way
To explain their shallow actions.

1/20/05

Paranoid fears of a man,
Who has seen them come
True, over and over again,
Through the cruel categorization
Of a stranger, who is condemned
To live in solitude farthest away
From bliss—they made you feel guilty
For far too long.

1/20/05

~~~~~~

A plea to catch a hold of the one
Whose dreams you want to make come true—
A love song for the times,
Addressed to someone who has
Your here inside her.
Allegedly, it happens to everyone
At some point in their lives.

1/20/05
~~~~~~

Begging turned into dependence
On someone who could save you
From the hatred you feel for
Those who have done you wrong.
Take her and wrap her up
In your eyes, lest her sunshine
Tries to get away.
These things repeated so many times
In history; tell them to the younger crowd
In so many words for them to relate.

1/20/05

People from the past still
Lingering in my life and doing
The things I have finished, or thought
I would have at my age.
One man told me that I was not the type
Who would easily be forgotten;
I suppose I should take it as a compliment.
Now my mind is stuck between the most
Recent years and how I have lived.
What kinds of things should I have
Done differently, and could these things
Have made me better off than I am today?
Unanswered questions, I suppose
That I would like to see many of them today
And let them know how I have changed
And broken through to the next chapter of my life
With flying colors that will hopefully see me
Through the last years of my youth.

(end of Elliott Smith poems)

1/20/05

Fallen Star

Just a child, yourself,
You were sent to discover
A different part of the world.
Now you think you're ready
To take on the burdens of the things
That I do not want to touch.
And, for that, people think I have fallen.
True, I do have yet to reach my
Full potential, but I have not fallen,
As you have said, because I have
Avoided your stereotypical way of life.
Not that you've really fallen,
But you've sacrificed your young life
As a part of the deal.
What has happened to the youth,
So jaded in some ways?

1/20/05

You ask me what is wrong
As I toss my head back and laugh;
As if the same question
Hadn't been asked of me
For years.
  They say, "Such a pity," and
I say, "This kind of thing is all too common."
You must not know me very well.

1/21/05

Winding down, this should not
Be happening right now; my legs
Should not feel so heavy.
I thought that I was young;
I thought I was allowing my body
To be as slim as it could.
Youth shall still be sprawled
All over my face, and the rest
Of my body should coordinate
Its function.
No more doubt!

1/21/05

This makes me go back—
Back to the days when I wasn't afraid
Of anything; especially my first
Great pride—my wonderful beauty
That would show that I have
Done something.
I am worth something in this world
Full of uncertainty.
Arouse the curiosity of those who
Questioned my ability before.
Set up a foundation and help me
Decide how I want to live.
So far, I like how it's turned out,
And I will become the girl in the book.
And the world (is) my attentive audience.
I don't have much else to say except
That it's about time.

1/21/05

The small of my back
Keeps getting larger.
Welcome, cavern!
Welcome because you have
Come a little late, but
That is better than nothing.
For things can only
Keep getting better.
My old, horrid self will be
Eradicated, and the lesser part
Of the public will ever know
It existed.

1/21/05

What the hell was I thinking,
What else could I have done
To prevent this insanity?
I can see myself in years gone by
And my kind deeds only
Putting me in jeopardy.
I knew that I should have
Cut myself off years ago,
But I never got the chance.
Will I ever get
To hide so far within myself
From the cruel madness?

1/23/05

Severed to the point
Of a mental coma,
Where I can think of nothing else
But the subject at hand.
Don't they know what they
Are doing to me; don't I know
What I'm doing to myself?
People should just let me be
When I said I have made up
My mind.
That's all there is to it
Because I can think of no other argument.

1/23/05

You dragged me out here,
Not out of my own accord.
So what else is new?
I must bring myself to bow
Down to you.
Things stick out in your mind—
Things that I, myself, would forget.
That's just how some minds work,
And mine is currently being
Dragged from its level of comfort.
It can't all be my fault.

1/23/05

Is Time the only thing
You want to get rid of,
Or is it my face?
I don’t know anymore,
And I may even decide
To help you along.
Every day, a haunting image
Looms in my mind, the
Precious thing I try to protect,
With every step of my being.
It is not working very well.

1/23/05

I knew your name
So many years ago,
When things didn't matter
Nearly as much.
My friend and I thought
We had everything
Planned out.
Those were the days;
Is there any way I can
Bring them back at a
Reasonable price?
Here I stand, on my knees,
Absorbing all the pain.

1/23/05

What do you think
She's up to?
I do not care, but you
Just might.
All the lies and the times
She disappeared,
How does it compare—
In the grand scheme of things?
Now you know that none
Of this really matters.

1/23/05

About the same girl.

I never knew who,

Until now.

Here is the basis

For part of your troubled life.

Such a shame—that a brilliant

Mind such as yours

Had to come from

The harsh realities of life.

1/23/05

The aching
In my head.
I wish the theme
From this song
Would be imbedded
In my mind.
After all, the alcohol
Has already gotten
To my brain.
I'm sure that many
Could relate to the
Bitter hate that resides
In my head.
Happened at one
Time or another,
Things that only
Make us more upset—
Happening right now.

1/23/05

I tried a drink
Very similar to yours
And was amazed at
What little it brought,
Even though it made
Me think of you
Almost the entire time.
Poor people trapped
In my mind,
With nowhere else to think.

1/23/05

~~~~~~

Such a tender creature,
What more can I say?
After all you've been through;
It's amazing that you're still here.

1/23/05
~~~~~~

When this used to
Come around, I had
No idea that life could
Be this troublesome,
This hard to comprehend
From the things that
Happen and the words
That fill our ears.
That's not to say that you
Didn't care at all;
Your art has touched me
And so many others.

1/23/05

Looking at the last remnants
Of the sun in the sky;
It is going west—going to
Put its troubles away.
Right now, I want to
Follow and see where
It leads—to the warm
Side of the sun, where everyone
Can go to be happy.

1/23/05

Playing until your fingers bleed;
What are you trying to prove?
I think I am beginning
To understand the things
That run around in circles,
Around your head—
A place that so many have
Feared and failed to
Understand.

1/23/05

Euphoria.
Running through my veins;
I can hardly hold the pen
In my hand.
If I could express myself
In any physical form,
I would run, leap, and play
To portray my message to people
In the world.
‘Tis true, ‘tis harder to write
When happiness circulates
Through every part of my body,
Like the sun burst in my soul,
And the torch is still in my heart.
Days surrounding, this makes up
For all the things that happened
In the latter part
Of last year.
Part of my victory comes
From knowing that the
Arrogant have been crushed.
But I rest my case because peace lies

In my heart, and my feet are dancing
To the same sweet tune, which has
Made me feel glad.
An earthly miracle helping me
To bring out the joy that's been
Missing for days—
I think I really needed this.

*dedicated to the New England Patriots and their victory over the Pittsburgh Steelers

1/23/05

When reduced to fear,
I take on this childlike state
That makes me think
I can hide from the world.
Sometimes, it works;
Sometimes, people may
Even forget my name.
Other times, they can
See through my façade,
Even though I don’t
Really want them to.
It all depends on the timing.

1/24/05

Things you would not
Take in vain because
It is not directed to you.
Nothing ever was; how
Sad all this may seem.
Who could have steered
You wrong and filled your mind
With these designed lies?
Ironic that all you do turns out
In the favor of others.

1/24/05

Television

Has taken my imagination

Away.

Through my own stupidity,

Laughter is the only thing

I can express, as I feel my soul

Being sucked down the tubes.

Comfort from this cold and bitter

World has gone too far to take me

Away from the things that I love.

1/25/05

My tired mind
Does not give me so much
As a revolutionary idea,
Tonight, when I am nearing
A denouement.
Each day presents a new beginning,
Which offers so many opportunities
For me to make something of myself
In this world.

1/25/05

A beloved man,
Who has entertained us
For years, has left
To watch us from the clouds,
While his memory lives on in the minds
Who knew him best.
(Announcing God with his humor)—
I wish that I could offer
More than this small tribute,
But I suppose he will be happy
To know that some
Unknown person cares.

*dedicated to Johnny Carson

1/25/05

Tabula rasa,

Empty tablet—

Doomed to repeat,

Until I can

Get some sleep…

1/25/05

This new obsession
Has come a little too late
Because I am involved
With someone else,
And you have already left.
I appreciated you before
But, right now, you have
Ironically come alive
So much after your
Parting work
To think that
I've supported you
All these years—gone before
I could read a story on your life.
I wish that I could have
Met you and shook your hand,
Even though I fear the impact
May not have been as great.
Your feelings toward people,
Sometimes, may have me questioning
Certain things.
We are only human and forced

To act under certain conditions.
 You needed guidance and were
Afraid to show it.
I'm sure that most any human being
Could relate.

*dedicated to Elliott Smith

1/26/05

My emotions would run wild,
Given what I am to face.
Months ago, I didn't know
Where I would be a year from now;
I still don't.
My fate in the hands of God
Because He knows what is best.
I am still trying to decide
What to do with myself.
And fear shall not overrun my life,
As I am still trying to find myself
In this vast world.

1/2705

I am not going to
Take this lying down.
Once I fade, they are
Not going to make a
Mockery of my age!
Every year, I shall look
Better than the year before,
And my health will be
Exquisite.
Any man with whom I'll
Be involved shall want
For nothing more, as my
Youthful attitude never
Leaves me, because it keeps
My persistent soul alive!

1/27/05

The eccentricities of people,
Such as myself, are brought
Out at awkward times.
Those (who are) scornful
Do not understand what
Lies behind these masterminds
That wield such power,
Confusing their owners
For at time.
How can cruelty compromise
The fact that some are jealous,
Or afraid; I don't believe
That it does.
I don't believe ridicule
Should be a part of these people's lives,
Since they feel so out of place already.

1/27/05

Such a mismatch
Are the two lovers,
Who want to confuse
And confound the world.
However, you cannot
Help but love them
In their tragic way.
They represent so many
Who feel that their relationships
Are always among the stormy waters.
Even though they eventually
Reached the calm, the storm
Started up again, and the
Vicious cycle continued until
It finally had to come to an end.

1/27/05

I heard a conversation
On the phone,
Saying that I was to go somewhere.
The excited words could not
Be quiet, as they leapt
Into my ear and prevented
My slumber from being
A great reality.
I suppose that it's time
I got out on my own,
To see what I can do
On this lonely planet.
Many would be sad to see
Me go, but I must keep
My head held high;
I must brave the storms so that
I can reap the rewards.
In this existence of man,
I must move ahead to take up
My duties, before
I further get consumed by the
Doubt and despair.

If my counterparts can do it,
Then why not me?
If nothing, I at least have
The training to move in the
Right direction, where everyone
Should go, given years of
Proper experience and guidance.

1/27/05

About time that you came to
A close so that I can move
On to another place, another chapter
To get prosperity.
Of course, there is always
Time to reminisce, but not
Everything should be spent
On recalling memories from the past.
Moving on, people still claim
That I am young—that I should
Take my chances while I still can.
Some of it has sunk into my head,
As I am still holding on tight.
I am not giving up on the
"Impossible dream" because
Time is on my side.
Though late to bloom,
I shall have what I desire,
As happiness fills my heart,
And I have amounted
To my full potential.
My self-worth rising

To the roof all because

I dared to change.

I dared to move on to make sure

My needs are me.

No more regrets;

Things will turn out for the best!

1/30/05

About the Author

Jen Selinsky was born in 1978 in Pittsburgh, PA. She was raised in Cranberry Township. In December 2004, Jen earned her MLS from Clarion University of Pennsylvania. She now lives in Sellersburg, IN.

Some of Jen's short works have been published in several anthologies, including *The Raider Review*, *Tobeco*, and *Essence of a Dream*, published by The National Library of Poetry—for which her poem, "Ode to the Forest," won an editor's choice award.

www.ingramcontent.com/pod-product-compliance
Lightning Source LLC
LaVergne TN
LVHW041032150826
845672LV00001B/286

* 9 7 9 8 6 5 2 7 7 1 5 5 3 *